Who Is
Maria
Tallchief?

Who Is
Maria
Tallchief?

by Catherine Gourley
illustrated by Val Paul Taylor

Grosset & Dunlap • New York

For my nieces Erika and Katrina,
dancers and actors both—C.G.

To Whitney, Stephanie and Haley.
May your light shine forever—VPT

Text copyright © 2002 by Catherine Gourley. Illustrations copyright © 2002 by Val Paul Taylor. Cover illustration copyright © 2002 by Nancy Harrison. All rights reserved. Published by Grosset & Dunlap, a division of Penguin Putnam Books for Young Readers, 345 Hudson Street, New York, NY 10014. GROSSET & DUNLAP is a trademark of Penguin Putnam Inc. Published simultaneously in Canada. Printed in the U.S.A.

Library of Congress Cataloging-in-Publication Data

Gourley, Catherine, 1950-
  Who is Maria Tallchief? / by Catherine Gourley ; illustrated by Val
Paul Taylor.
    p. cm. — (Who was— ?)
  Summary: A biography of the Osage Indian ballerina whose love of dance
took her from a life on a reservation to a career on the stage.
  1. Tallchief, Maria—Juvenile literature. 2. Ballerinas—United
States—Biography—Juvenile literature. 3. Indian ballerinas—United
States—Biography—Juvenile literature. 4. Osage Indians—United
States—Biography—Juvenile literature. [1. Tallchief, Maria. 2. Ballet
dancers. 3. Osage Indians—Biography. 4. Indians of North
America—Biography. 5. Women—Biography.] I. Taylor, Val Paul, ill. II.
Title. III. Series.
GV1785.T32 G68 2002
792.8'028'092—dc21

2002003909

ISBN 0-448-42675-7 (pbk)   A B C D E F G H I J
ISBN 0-448-42831-8 (GB)   A B C D E F G H I J

Contents

Who Is
Maria Tallchief?

Maria Tallchief was a ballerina, but she was not just another toe-dancer. She was America's first *prima ballerina*. A prima ballerina is the star of the show, the very best dancer on the stage. Maria danced for kings and queens and presidents. She thrilled her audiences with amazing leaps and arabesques. Her performances as a swan queen, a sugar plum fairy, and a magical firebird stand out as some of

Osage Reservation

TULSA

OKLAHOMA

the most beautiful chapters in American ballet history.

She was a Native American, the daughter of a full-blooded Osage. Maria's story begins on the Osage reservation in the rolling hills of northeastern Oklahoma. As a child, the beat of the tom-toms excited her. The rhythm of the drums filled the hollow of her bones. The songs of her people's past woke within her a love of dance and the prima ballerina she would one day become.

Chapter 1
The Osage Reservation

Maria opened her eyes. She had fallen asleep in the living room, and now her father was carrying her upstairs. She snuggled closer against his warm body and stared at his shiny black hair. His dark eyes smiled down at Maria.

Maria's first memory was that tender moment, waking to find herself safe in her father's arms. She was three years old, and her father seemed like a giant to her. Alexander Joseph Tall Chief was six feet two inches. He had broad shoulders and a swaggering confidence that had won the heart of Ruth Porter, a farm girl from Kansas. He was Osage. She was Scottish and Irish. They were married soon after meeting in the small town of Fairfax, Oklahoma.

Maria came into the world on a cold winter day, January 24, 1925. Her parents named her Betty Marie, after her two grandmothers, Elizabeth, "Eliza," Tall Chief and Marie Porter. Maria had an older brother named Jerry. When Maria was almost two years old, her sister Marjorie was born. The Tall Chief family lived in a ten-room, red-brick house on a hill overlooking the Osage reservation.

The Osage hills were a magical place for Maria. The prairie grasses bowed their heads and whispered in the wind. Wildflowers bloomed goldenrod yellow and daisy white. Butterflies and the songs of meadowlarks filled the air. In summer, Maria hunted through the high grasses for arrowheads.

The sharp tips of stone were bits of Osage history. Whenever she found one, she said, shivers raced up her spine.

The Osage had lived on the plains of North America for many hundreds of years. Before the white settlers came, the prairie was a sea of grasses so tall that an Osage hunter had to stand on the back of his pony to see what lay beyond. The brown clouds and thunder in the distance were herds of buffalo. The

Osage called these bearded animals "brothers."

The white settlers, whom the Osage called "Heavy Eyebrows," changed the land and the lives of the native people forever. Heavy Eyebrows plowed under the sweet-smelling grasses to farm the land. They slaughtered and skinned the buffalo, sending the woolly hides back East on the railroads that they had built across the plains. In some places along the iron rails, mounds of buffalo bones rose almost as high as the ancient prairie grasses.

The government of the white settlers forced the Osage onto reservations, first in the country Heavy Eyebrows called Kansas, then to a new place called Oklahoma. The Osage were hunters and gatherers. Without the buffalo, they could not hunt. Heavy Eyebrows wanted the Osage to become farmers. Year after year they scratched a living from the baked-red soil, but the crops they grew were not enough. The Osage were a proud people. Now they were starving. They had

Old Osage Village

Teepee

Scraping Buffalo Hides

Gardens

no choice but to accept the handouts of food and supplies from the white government agents.

Maria's ancestors had a belief, however—an ancient prophecy. One day, great wealth would return to the Osage. At the start of the twentieth century, the prophecy came true. Beneath the whispering grasses, miles below the rolling hills of northeastern Oklahoma, was a lake of black gold—oil. The discovery of oil on the reservation made the Osage people the wealthiest Native American tribe in the country. Soon, hundreds of oil derricks were pumping the black gold to the surface. By the time

Maria was born, these clanking and hissing metal skeletons had replaced the humped-back buffalo on the prairie of Oklahoma.

Oil saved the Osage people from starvation. But oil also brought trouble, especially to the Tall Chief family.

Chapter 2
The Rampage

Maria's father was not wealthy, but he was well-to-do. "We didn't live in a teepee," Maria often told people who asked about her life on the reservation. "And we were never hungry."

Maria's father owned a movie theater and a pool hall on the main street in town, but those businesses did not earn much money for the family. Instead, her father depended for money on the oil companies. They paid him for the right to drill oil on his land. Often, when a check for hundreds

of dollars arrived, he pocketed the money and disappeared for days. Ruth Tall Chief did not know where her husband was, but she knew what he was doing: drinking. As much as a week might pass before he returned home.

Maria remembered how frightened her mother became during those "binges." When Maria's father drank, he got mean. "The walls seemed to shake and the air seemed to fill with the thunder of his fury," Maria remembered.

Her mother tried to reason with him. "You are throwing away the money your family needs to live!" How was she to feed her daughters? she asked.

The giant towered over his wife. His dark eyes were not kind now. They were angry. "I'm tired of hearing about money!" he shouted. He swung his arm, sweeping a stack of books from the table. They crashed to the floor.

Maria grabbed Marjorie's hand, and together the sisters ran down the hill to Grandma Tall

Chief's house. Maria cried for her to come quickly and save her mother!

Her father's "rampage," as Maria called it, ended without violence. She never once saw her father strike her mother. Still, a few months later when the next oil check arrived, her father disappeared again. Oil might have saved the Osage from starving, but it could not restore her father's lost pride. Maria did not know what dark thoughts clouded her father's mind during his binges. In time, however, she came to understand what her mother already knew. Her father was an alcoholic.

One day Maria would write a book about her life. "I idolized him," Maria wrote about her father. "But while we were growing up, he was often unbearable."

Chapter 3
The Keeper of the Drum

Maria learned about her Osage heritage from her grandmother. Eliza Tall Chief wore her black hair in a long braid, as was the custom for Osage women. She wrapped her shoulders in a colorfully striped tribal blanket. She told stories of the past. Many, many years ago, Maria's great-grandfather, Chief Peter Bigheart, had traveled to Washington, D.C., to work with the white government leaders in planning the Osage reservation. Grandma Tall Chief also spoke of the powwow, a great festival that was very important to the Osage people.

Belt

Each spring, Grandma Tall Chief said, the Osage held a powwow. The women wore their finest shirts and wide-beaded belts. They rubbed chalky gypsum over their doeskin leggings. Silver and turquoise bracelets ringed their arms. The dancing

Bracelet

began in the afternoon and lasted for hours, Grandma Tall Chief said. Only the men danced. They fastened hawkbells around their legs below their knees. As the men raised one leg, then the other, the bells jingle-jangled. The men didn't dress in feather bonnets. They didn't spin or flail their arms. The Osage danced with dignity, Grandma Tall Chief said.

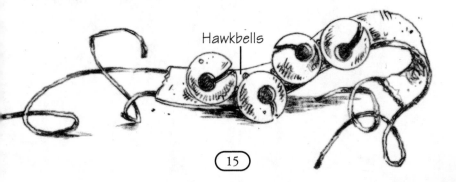

Hawkbells

One June afternoon, Daddy took Maria and
Marjorie to a powwow. This was even more exciting

Osage Dancers
Men in inner circle

Drummers

for Maria than finding arrowheads in the grass.
The Osage sat in semicircles. Their tribal blankets

Women on outside

covered their shoulders. Just as Grandma Tall Chief had said, the women in their moccasins and silver jewelry did not dance. "Instead," Maria remembered, "they formed a circle around the men and did a little side step, shifting their weight from one foot to the other in time with the drumbeat."

The keeper of the drum was a boy. The Osage always chose a boy for this honor, Grandma Tall Chief had explained. His beating on the kettledrum brought honor to his family.

The men sang as they danced. The stories they sang told of times long ago and were as important as the dance itself. The story *was* the dance—mysterious and solemn. The men circled the large drum in the center of the dance ground. When the drumbeats stopped, each dancer froze, an uplifted foot in midair. Maria was entranced.

Even as the sun slipped closer to the sandstone hills, the drumming and the dancing continued. In the shadows, the blackjack trees bending over the stream could have been the ghosts of Maria's Osage ancestors.

"The powwow was a journey to the past," Maria said. She never forgot the rhythm of those ancient songs. One day, in her own way, she would become a sort of keeper of the drum. Through dance and story, Maria would bring honor to her family and to the Osage people.

Chapter 4
Pianos and Toe Shoes

As a child, Maria thought of herself as a "typical Indian girl." She was shy and polite and eager to please the adults in her life. Her brother Jerry, however, had a terrible temper like his father. Maria sometimes fought with Jerry. Mostly, she simply ran away from him.

Maria's mother explained to her daughters that Jerry's problems began when he was just four years old. A horse kicked him in the head. Although Jerry seemed to recover, he could not learn the alphabet. He could not read, no matter how many times Ruth pointed and repeated the letters for him. One day, unable to control Jerry's outbursts, Maria's parents decided to send him away to a military school.

Now that Jerry had left home, Ruth Tall Chief turned all her attention to her two daughters. One day, she promised herself, she would take her girls away from the reservation and the small town of Fairfax with its clanking oil derricks and dusty roads. She would take them away from their father's frightening binges fueled by oil money. Her girls would perform on stage and become famous. Traditional Indian dancing was not what Ruth Tall Chief had in mind, either. Her girls would dance ballet. During the summer when Maria was three years old, her mother took her for her

first lesson. When Marjorie was three, she too began her lessons.

Maria's best friend was her sister. She and Marjorie dressed alike. They did everything together, including learning how to dance. In Fairfax, their teacher was a woman who knew very little about ballet. Mrs. Sabin didn't teach the Tall Chief girls the basic positions and movements. She forced five-year-old Maria to go up on her toes before her feet were strong enough to hold her. Mrs. Sabin did not know that dancing *en pointe* too early could damage forever a little girl's feet.

Ruth bought satin toe shoes in sizes too large for her girls. That way, they didn't out-grow their dancing slippers so quickly. She stuffed the toes of the slippers with cotton. Pain needled Maria's feet whenever she stood *en pointe.* She never told her mother about the pain.

Ruth sewed the costumes for her daughters' dance routines. For one patriotic dance routine, Ruth made Maria a cape and sewed an American flag on the inside lining. On stage as the record "Stars and Stripes Forever" played, Maria twirled and twirled—sometimes on her toes and sometimes not—until she was dizzy.

A dancer must know music, and so Ruth also hired a piano teacher. While other children played

outside after school, Maria now practiced both her piano lessons and her dance steps. Ruth watched her daughters closely. She saw that Marjorie could extend her leg almost to her head. That was much

higher than Maria could. On the other hand, Maria could close her eyes and listen to a melody, then immediately identify the notes. "That's a C, that's a G," she'd tell the piano teacher. Then she played the same melody without making a mistake.

"Your daughter has perfect pitch," the piano teacher told Maria's mother. It was a remarkable musical talent.

Ruth began to imagine different futures for her daughters. One day Marjorie would become a ballerina. Maria would become a concert pianist. For now, however, the two sisters continued to dance together. Sometimes they performed on stage in their father's movie theater. More often, they performed at county fairs, Boy Scout jamborees, and rodeos.

The rodeo especially frightened Maria. The long-horned bulls in their pens snorted and pawed the dirt. The muscles along their flanks quivered nervously. Behind the grandstand, Maria heard the cowboys talking. Riding a rodeo bull, they said, was like riding a ton of swirling fury. The worst thing was getting stepped on. If a bull got the chance, said the cowboys, it would run you over for sure!

Like the bulls in their pens, Maria waited nervously for her turn to go into the arena to entertain

the audience. She preferred dancing in Daddy's theater. At least in the movie house, a snorting swirl of fury could not run her over!

Often while traveling to and from the county fairs and rodeos, Ruth complained to her husband. If they stayed on the reservation, she said, her girls would never achieve greatness. And she was certain that greatness was in them. They would dance at county fairs and rodeos in homemade costumes all their lives. In California, they would have a better life. At last, Joseph Tall Chief agreed.

In 1933, when Maria was eight years old, the Tall Chief family packed up their belongings and moved to Los Angeles. If Maria felt sad leaving the Osage hills and her Grandma Tall Chief behind, once again she did not complain.

Chapter 5
Madame Nijinska

California was full of colors that Maria had never seen in Oklahoma—groves of bright oranges, apricots, and peaches. The Pacific Ocean shimmered a silvery blue in the sunshine. Even her father seemed happier. He could golf every day!

Maria and Marjorie began their ballet lessons right away. Ernest Belcher welcomed the two girls

into his class. He was shocked to learn that both Maria and Marjorie had been dancing on their toes for years. It was a miracle, he told Ruth, that both girls had not injured themselves. "Forget everything

Mrs. Sabin showed you," he told his new pupils. "You must start all over and learn the basic steps."

THE BASIC STEPS

First position   Second position

Third position   Fourth position   Fifth position

Ballet school was hard work, but Maria was happy in Mr. Belcher's class. She was not so happy in Beverly Vista School, however. She could read far better than the other students in the third grade, so she was often bored with the lessons.

When she came into the classroom, the students covered their mouths with their hands and made war whoops. Where were her feathers? they teased. Did she live in a teepee? Was her last name Tall or was it Chief? How many scalps had her father taken?

It didn't help much either when Ruth decided her girls would begin performing again at county fairs. She thought their Osage heritage would make them a more interesting act. She sewed new costumes—buckskins with fringe, headbands with feathers, and hawkbells down the outside of each leg. Maria disliked the costume, but she disliked the dance routine even more. Osage women did not dance. Only men wore the traditional hawk-bells. Grandma Tall Chief knew that. Why didn't

her mother understand? Maria was proud of her Osage heritage, but this dance seemed all wrong.

Ruth was determined. As long as the costumes fit, her daughters would dance to the tom-toms. As always, Maria did as she was told. The one thing Maria could change, however, was her name. She began to write Tallchief as one word, not two. Maybe *that* would stop some of the teasing.

When Maria was twelve—and the dreaded buckskin costume no longer fit—she met a woman who changed her life forever. The woman's name was Madame Nijinska, and she became Maria's new ballet instructor.

Madame was short and round. Her large green eyes were hawk-like. She missed nothing. And she was demanding. Her pupils took their place at a long rail called the "barre" to begin their exercises. Madame's hard fingers rapped

Maria's shoulder. Hold your elbow this way, she instructed. Use your back muscles. Over and over again she corrected Maria's movements.

Madame herself danced for them, showing them the proper way to move their feet. Mrs. Sabin had never danced. Mr. Belcher had never danced. As she watched Madame Nijinska, Maria suddenly knew what she wanted. Maria had perfect pitch in playing the piano. Now she wanted to be perfect on the dance floor, too. Practice was no longer just an hour or two a day. Maria began to live and breathe ballet, because that was how Madame said it must be.

"When you sleep, sleep like ballerina," Madame told Maria in her Russian accent. "Even on street waiting for bus, stand like ballerina."

When Maria was fifteen, Madame Nijinska announced that she would stage three ballets.

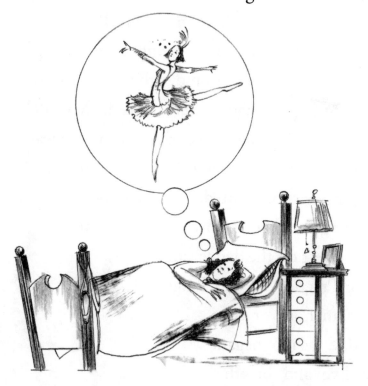

One of the ballets was *Chopin Concerto*. It was a classical piece that Maria had learned to play on the piano. Maria knew the music in her soul. She was certain that she was Madame's favorite pupil.

That was why she was so crushed when she did not get the lead role. Madame cast her as one of the "corps." The corps is a group of dancers who move together on stage. No one dances alone. No one rises *en pointe* or leaps unless all the others do. Everyone does the same thing at the same time.

Ruth saw the hurt in her daughter's eyes. She saw, too, that Maria would never become a concert pianist. Dancing had become Maria's dream. Ruth comforted her daughter. "You have to show that you want to dance with all your heart, even in the corps. You shouldn't just expect a role to be handed to you."

It was an important lesson for Maria. "The next day," she said, "I put everything into rehearsing. I went over the steps day and night."

Madame noticed Maria's dedication, and she smiled. Her favorite pupil was indeed learning. One day, she might even become a star.

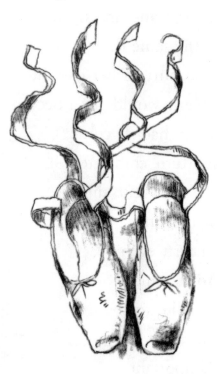

Chapter 6
On the Road

When Maria graduated from high school in 1942, her father told her it was time that she began earning a living. Maria's first paid job was dancing in a movie. It was a musical called *Presenting Lily Mars*. The star of the movie was a young actress named Judy Garland. While Maria was intrigued by the movie star, the dancing job

was not very challenging. Maria's heart simply wasn't in Hollywood. She wanted to become a ballerina.

Earlier in the year, Maria had seen the Ballet Russe de Monte Carlo perform. This was a dance company that traveled across the country. Some of the lead dancers had even joined one of Madame's classes to work with her best pupils. Maria was among them.

Once again, Maria's mother came up with a plan. She arranged for Maria to travel with a friend to New York City. Once there, Maria could audition for the Ballet Russe.

Maria was seventeen years old that summer of 1942. America was at war with Japan and Germany. The train terminal was crowded with soldiers hugging their wives and kissing their children goodbye. Maria had never traveled alone anywhere. She could not remember a time when Marjorie was not at her side. But her sister was still in high school and had to stay behind.

"All aboard!" the train conductor called. Maria hugged her family, then she stepped onto the train.

Once she arrived in New York City a few days later, Maria faced a great disappointment. The

NEW YORK CITY

secretary of the Ballet Russe turned her away. "We don't need any more dancers," the woman said coldly.

The words tore at Maria's heart. She had traveled all the way across the country with the hope of joining the Ballet Russe. She swallowed back  her tears long enough to write her name and the address of her hotel in New York City. She gave it to the secretary. Once outside, Maria began to cry. She was alone and lonely in the city, and she didn't have a job.

Three days later, something wonderful happened. Mr. Denham, who was the head of the Ballet Russe, remembered Maria. He had seen her dance when the Ballet Russe had visited Madame Nijinska's studio a year earlier. Now the company was about to go on tour. At the last minute, one of his dancers had decided to leave the company. Mr. Denham hired Maria.

A few days later, Maria once again arrived at the train station dragging her heavy suitcase behind her. A crowd of dancers and musicians was already on the platform. Maria knew no one. She took a seat in the train car. All night, she sat upright in the darkened car, because she didn't know—as the other, more-experienced travelers did—how to make her seat recline. And she was too timid to ask for help. In the morning, her back and legs were stiff. What did it matter? She was going to dance with the Ballet Russe!

In each city, the troupe unloaded its costumes and musical instruments. The dancers went first to the theater where they would perform that evening. Because of the long hours cramped on a train or sometimes a bus, they carefully stretched their legs and arms and back. After warming up, they took a class. Then they went to their hotel rooms. Often, the rooms were shabby, small, and dark. The girls paid for their rooms out of their weekly earnings. To save money, three girls shared a room. Sometimes, Maria slept on a mattress. Other nights, she slept on the floor. The dancers took turns washing their hair in the bathroom sink down the hall. Refreshed, they returned to the theater to rehearse again before the evening's performance.

A choreographer plans the dance steps in a ballet. Often, the choreographer instructed the dancers to learn new roles during the day for a performance that night. Learning new roles exhausted Maria. She lost weight. And always, her hands and feet were like ice.

"Maria, you must eat," Mr. Denham scolded her. "A dancer must keep her strength."

Maria promised to eat more. She didn't tell him, however, that she could barely afford a plate of spaghetti for twenty-five cents. Sometimes, as a special treat, Maria bought Fig Newton cookies. Most weeks, her mother sent her a five-dollar bill. Maria refused to spend that money on food. It was her savings! She locked it safely away in her suitcase.

When she was rehearsing, food and money were the last things on Maria's mind. Her willingness to learn caught the eye of the choreographer. Soon, he cast her as an understudy for one of the ballerinas. If the ballerina could not perform, then Maria would take her place on stage.

The ballerina was shocked. "Maria? She is too young. She is not ready. It is a mistake."

Maria feared the ballerina was right. Some nights, Maria worried so much that she could not sleep. What if she had to dance the ballerina's role and she failed? She would embarrass the entire dance company. Yet whatever her fears, she resolved to go on stage and show what she could do.

Many of the dancers in the Ballet Russe were Russian. For them, ballet was a Russian art. The Americans were merely imitators. That seventeen-

year-old Maria had come so far so quickly made some of the Russians jealous. During a rehearsal, Maria's Russian partner let go of her hand at the wrong moment, and she fell. She could have been seriously injured. Had he done it on purpose? She had no way of knowing.

"You should change your name to Tallchieva," Mr. Denham told her one day. He felt Tallchieva sounded Russian. People admired Russian dancers much more than American dancers. Look at all the famous Russian prima ballerinas, he said. America had no prima ballerinas.

Maria remembered the schoolchildren whose war whoops had made her feel like an outcast. She was proud to be Osage. She was proud also to be an American. No, she decided, she would never change her name again just to fit in.

During Maria's first year with the Ballet Russe, she danced as one of the corps. Someday, she hoped to dance in a leading role. For now, she was happy just to be part of the company that included such wonderful Russian ballerinas as Alexandra Danilova and Nathalie Krassovska.

In May of 1943, Nathalie and Mr. Denham had an argument. Nathalie walked out of the theater and did not return. Maria never learned what the argument was about. All she knew was that she was to dance in Nathalie's place. The time had come for Maria to step from the corps into the spotlight as a soloist. She was terrified.

THE BALLET COMPANY

Although dancers study ballet for many years before joing a company, they still have much to learn about dancing technique. As dancers learn and improve, they advance from the corps to soloist, from ballerina to prima ballerina.

Corps de ballet

Most dancers begin as members of the corps. They dance together as one group, everybody moving the same way at the same time. In a ballet like *The Nutcracker*, they are the guests who attend the holiday party. In *Sleeping Beauty*, they are the villagers.

Coryphees

This is a small group of dancers, quite often six. The choreographer plans their steps, and they perform together as semi-soloists.

The Soloist

As a dancer learns or improves upon technique, the choreographer may promote the dancer to the position of soloist. A soloist dances alone on stage. Some soloists become "principal" dancers with a company. That means they will dance in leading roles.

THE BALLET COMPANY

The Ballerina

After much hard work and many performances, a principal dancer may rise even higher to the position of ballerina. A ballerina is not only a very accomplished dancer but also one who dances with passion and artistic feeling.

The Prima Ballerina

Only a few ballerinas will become prima ballerinas. She is much more than just a star. Her performances are nearly perfect and bring fame not just to herself but to the entire ballet company.

The ballet that Maria performed was the one that she knew and loved so much, *Chopin Concerto*. She had been practicing the dance steps ever since the choreographer had made her an understudy.

"The moment of truth had arrived," Maria would say later. She stepped on stage. Later that

night, sitting in her dressing room with a bouquet of flowers, Maria could hardly remember the performance. It just seemed to "fly by," she said.

A few weeks later, Maria performed the same ballet in New York City. In the audience was John Martin, a dance critic for *The New York Times*. He

later wrote this about Maria: *Tallchief is the real discovery in the classic field . . . When she has grown up, so to speak, she can hardly escape being Somebody.*

Maria was grown up. She was eighteen years old. But in the dance world, she was a newcomer. She still had much to learn. She had no way of knowing that within a few months she would meet the person who would teach her everything she needed to know about ballet. His name was George Balanchine.

Chapter 7
Mr. Balanchine's Muse

George Balanchine was the new choreographer for the Ballet Russe. Every day, he watched Maria closely. One time she was doing exercises at the barre. Her right hand lightly held the rail as she slowly slid her left foot across the floor, pointing the toes. The exercise is called *battement tendu*. Finally, the new choreographer stepped forward. "If only you would learn to do *battement tendu* properly," he said, "you wouldn't have to learn anything else."

His words crushed her. She felt as if she were still a child who had to relearn *once again* the basics of ballet.

In the ballet world, some people thought George Balanchine was a genius while others

thought him cold
and unemotional.
Maria had seen him
work with dancers.
He created magic
on the stage.

Madame Nijinska had given Maria a passion for ballet. Mr. Balanchine, another Russian, could give her discipline. With his help, she began to retrain her legs to move more precisely.

During the day, she took classes. In the evening, she danced. Months passed. The changes in her body surprised her. Her legs seemed longer. Her muscles had stretched. Even her neck seemed more gracefully long. As her dancing improved, her confidence in herself soared.

Mr. Balanchine's interest in Maria was more than just professional. He was falling in love with her. One night, he asked her to marry him. Maria was unable to speak. Mr. Balanchine was twenty years older than she! And he had been married and divorced, not once but twice! Her mother and father would never approve of such a marriage.

The Russian was very handsome with his dark eyes. In the weeks that followed, Maria began to feel as if she were living in a ballet fairy tale. She was Sleeping Beauty or Cinderella. Mr. Balanchine was her handsome "prince of dance."

They married in the summer of 1946 in New York City. The bride was twenty-one years old. Just as Maria had predicted, her mother and father did not come to the wedding. Nor was Marjorie there. Maria's sister had graduated from high school and joined a different ballet company. She was performing and could not get away. Even though Maria missed her family, she felt real joy when George slipped the wedding ring onto her finger. She and George had each other, and that was all that truly mattered.

"You are my muse, my inspiration," George told his young wife. In Greek mythology, a muse

is a goddess who sparks the imagination of an
artist or a poet. George used music and dance to
create great works of art. With Maria as his muse,
he began choreographing new ballets just for her.

He was patient but demanding. "Do it over
again, this way," he told Maria. He danced the

steps himself so she could see exactly how he wished her to move. Maria had always been eager to please. If George believed she could make a grand *jeté*, or jump, then she would try with all her strength and concentration to do what he wished. When she succeeded, he simply smiled and said, "I knew all along you could do it."

Grand jeté

In 1947, George accepted a temporary job as the choreographer for the Paris Opera Ballet. Maria traveled by ship to France to be with him. She would also dance with the ballet company under her husband's direction.

One of the ballets they rehearsed was *Apollo*. The subject of the ballet is the Greek god Apollo and the nine muses who inspire works of art. The ballerina Tamara Toumanova had the lead role of Terpsichore, the muse who inspired mortals in the art of dance. A few weeks before the opening night, Tamara became ill. George decided Maria would take Tamara's place.

Apollo

At first, Maria questioned her husband's decision. Tamara Toumanova was famous. In contrast, no one in Paris had ever heard of Maria Tallchief. In fact, no American ballerina had ever danced before at the Paris Opera House.

George was determined. Maria was his muse, and she would dance as Terpsichore.

On opening night, the King and Queen of Sweden were in the audience. As Maria waited nervously in the wings for the curtain to rise, she wondered if the audience would accept her, a shy girl from the Osage reservation in Oklahoma. She need not have worried.

The next morning, Maria's photograph appeared in the Paris newspapers. One headline read: *Peau rouge danse à l'Opera pour le Roi de Suede!* In English it meant, Red skin dances at the Opera House for the King of Sweden!

Maria had never forgotten the war whoops of her classmates. But she was older now. She understood that the French had not meant to insult her by calling her a "red skin." They were simply fascinated by her Native American heritage. Even George sometimes teased her. He called her his "Pocahontas," after the Indian princess in American history who saved the life of a white man, John Smith.

Maria understood the fascination, but she was also determined. If she were to become a prima ballerina, then it must be because of her dancing and not because of the color of her skin.

The Balanchines returned to America in the fall of 1947. Six months in Paris had changed both Maria and George. Maria had new confidence in herself as a dancer. George had a new dream. He wanted to start a ballet company. Instead of spotlighting dancers from Europe, his company would train American dancers. One year later, the dream became real. The New York City Ballet gave its first performance.

GEORGE BALANCHINE

George Balanchine was born in Russia in 1904. Like Maria, he began studying dance when he was still a child. Because the ballet school in St. Petersburg was far from George's home, he lived at the school and not with his parents. As a young man, he joined the Soviet State Ballet, also known as the Kirov Ballet.

George Balanchine

Although George performed on stage, his real love was choreography. He had new ideas about how dancers should move on stage. Most ballets told stories, but George believed that the music of the ballet was more important than the story. So he created ballets where the dancers interpreted the music.

The Russian ballet company for whom Balanchine worked did not like his ideas. They dismissed him.

George left Russia. He traveled throughout Europe, dancing and choreographing. While looking for work in London, England, George met a wealthy American named Lincoln Kirstein. The two became friends and business partners. George traveled to America and, with Lincoln's help, began to choreograph plays on Broadway in New York City and movie musicals in Hollywood.

Like Maria, George's true love was ballet. At the time he met Maria Tallchief, George Balanchine was already famous. Some people thought him a genius; others thought him as hard and demanding as an army general.

George Balanchine once said that ballet is woman. In Maria Tallchief, he found not just a devoted wife but also a muse. She became his inspiration, and together they made ballet history.

George Balanchine's new company was small and didn't have much money. Even so, George vowed to make the New York City Ballet the best dance company in America. For the next three years, both he and Maria worked very hard. She danced in her husband's ballets. She danced also in ballets staged by other dance companies. The dance critics were paying more attention to Mr. Balanchine's ballerina.

"Maria Tallchief can make everything she does on stage look glittery," a dance critic wrote. "Some dancers are pearls," wrote another critic. "Maria Tallchief is a diamond."

Maria longed to be perfect if not for her own sake, then for George's. And yet, not every performance went well. Maria never forgot the first time she danced as the white swan maiden, Odette, in *Swan Lake*. It was the winter of 1949. Maria had difficulty concentrating. Another dancer, playing Benno, knelt before her. She balanced one foot on his thigh, raising her leg behind her and extending her hand to her partner, "Prince Siegfried." Suddenly her leg trembled. She fell forward. The next moment, the swan queen, her prince and Benno were sprawled ungracefully on the floor.

Maria was mortified. There was nothing she could do except stand up and continue dancing.

After the performance, Maria felt miserable. George was kind. He did not scold her. Still, Maria believed she had let him down. She had danced badly.

Late that night, a friend telephoned her. "I just want you to know, Maria, maybe you're not too happy tonight about your performance," she said. "But it was nerves."

Maria's mood brightened a little. Her friend had reminded her of an important truth in ballet: No one—not even the great Balanchine's wife—could be perfect every time.

Chapter 8
The Firebird's Magic

The applause for Maria Tallchief grew louder with each new ballet George created for her. In 1949, just months before her twenty-fifth birthday, George challenged Maria once again. He created a new ballet just for her, *The Firebird*. In this performance, Maria would play a mythical creature from Russian folklore.

The story begins in an enchanted garden where Prince Ivan discovers a rare and beautiful firebird. Ivan chases and then captures the creature. The frightened firebird pleads for her freedom. Finally, Ivan agrees. The grateful firebird gives the prince one of her blazing feathers, and she promises that if Ivan is ever in trouble, he may use the feather to call for her help. Too soon, Ivan does indeed find himself in need of the firebird's magic. The princess he loves has fallen under the spell of an evil magician. Ivan calls upon the firebird to help

save his love. As in all fairy tales, good triumphs over evil. Ivan and the princess marry, and the fire-bird flies away, a free creature once again.

The role of the firebird terrified Maria. George had choreographed truly amazing leaps as the bird tries to avoid capture. George wanted to show off Maria's technical abilities. Yet, even he was nervous. So many things had already gone wrong. During one rehearsal, Maria leaped into her partner's arms with such force that she nearly knocked him to the floor.

As opening night approached, Maria became ill. She was cold and tired. Each time she swallowed, her throat felt as if it were on fire. This was more than nerves! George took her to the doctor. The doctor announced that Maria's tonsils were infected. She must have an operation to remove them. "But I cannot have an operation," Maria argued. "I must dance!"

The doctor insisted.

After the surgery, he ordered Maria to stay in bed and sleep. For two days, Maria tried to rest. Always, her mind drifted back to that mythical

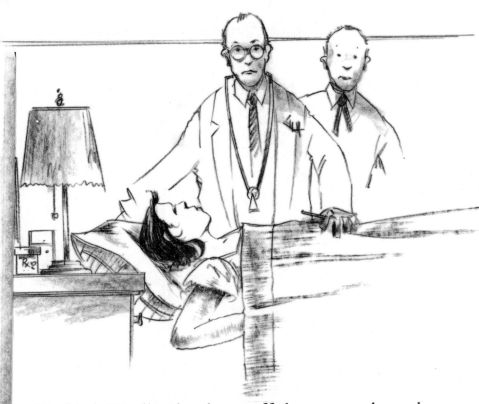

Firebird. Finally, she threw off the covers, dressed in her leotards, and returned to the rehearsals.

On the day of the opening night's performance, Maria's costume finally arrived. The headdress was a crown of feathers. Maria had not yet danced in the crown. How might it affect her balance, her *jetés*? There was no time to rehearse. Someone hurriedly pinned the feathered crown onto Maria's head.

Waiting in the wings, Maria felt her heart flutter. She had never been so nervous before a performance. The orchestra began to play.

As the curtain rose, Maria took a deep breath. The ballerina who stepped on stage was no longer Maria Tallchief. She was a mythical, magical bird with feathers ablaze.

Ordinarily, George would have worn his blue suit or his fancy white dinner jacket to the opening night's performance. He did not expect curtain calls tonight, so he had arrived at the theater wearing rather ordinary clothes. As he watched Maria's performance and heard the gasps of amazement from the audience, George realized that he had been wrong. Maria's frightened bird now fluttered, now flashed, now seemingly flew through the air into her partner's arms.

When the curtain fell at the end of the performance, something truly magical happened. The people in the audience rose to their feet and roared with excitement as if they weren't at a ballet at all but at a football game! They chanted over and over, "Tallchief! Tallchief! Tallchief!"

Backstage, Maria was confused. She had not practiced a curtain call, but clearly the audience was demanding that she return to the stage. They were on their feet, shouting and applauding. "As long as I live," Maria would one day write, "I'll never forget the roar."

That night, Maria's dream came true. She had become America's *prima ballerina*.

Chapter 9
Princess of Two Worlds

Maria loved dancing. The applause and cheers of the audiences thrilled her. Even so, she wanted something more. She wanted to have a child. George loved children, but he did not want to have any of his own. Children would complicate their busy lives, he said.

Marjorie and her husband

Maria also missed her sister. Marjorie had married a dancer. Both she and her husband had joined a ballet company in Europe. Maria hardly ever saw her sister.

For another year,

Maria and George lived and worked together. Maria wasn't unhappy, but she wasn't complete, either. Finally, in 1951, Maria and George ended their five-year marriage. But they did not end their artistic relationship. Maria was still George's muse. He continued to create ballets for her. And she continued to dance for him.

A year later, Maria fell in love again. At least, she thought it was love. Elmourza Natirboff was an airplane pilot. He knew nothing about ballet. Maria didn't care. Elmourza was handsome and fun to be with. They went to horse races and parties. After a whirlwind romance, they married. Then, just as quickly, the marriage began to unravel.

Elmourza did not understand the long hours his wife's career demanded. He didn't understand why she was so exhausted after a performance. He also had a temper. One night, angry at her about something she didn't quite understand, Elmourza kicked a wastebasket across the room. Suddenly, Maria remembered her father's angry outbursts during his drinking binges. Maria did not want to live the life her mother had in Fairfax. Maria left Elmourza, ending their short but troubled marriage.

In June of 1953, Maria returned to the Osage reservation in Oklahoma. Her people had called her home to honor her. On Main Street, people lined the sidewalks. They waved American flags. Signs in storefronts read, *Welcome home, Maria!* Their kindness overwhelmed her.

She entered her father's movie theater where she and Marjorie had danced in their first recitals.

Maria's parents were there. So was Grandma Tall Chief. Her hair, graying now, still hung in a braid down her back. A tribal blanket still hugged her shoulders.

Today, however, Maria would not dance. Today, she was the guest of honor. The Tribal Council welcomed her into the Osage tribe, giving her the name that Grandma Tall Chief had chosen for her: Princess Wa-Xthe-Thonba. It meant "Princess of Two Worlds." The chief placed a feathered bonnet on Maria's head. She was more accustomed to diamond tiaras, and the heavy headdress felt awkward.

Afterward, Maria returned to the red brick house on the hill overlooking the reservation. That afternoon in the Osage hills, America's prima ballerina feasted on the traditional Osage foods she had loved as a child: fried squaw bread and dried corn boiled with beef. If only for one day, Maria was once again that shy Indian girl who hunted for arrowheads in the long, whispering grasses.

Chapter 10
New Loves and Sad Farewells

In 1953, Maria was the most famous ballerina in the world. She met the president of the United States, Dwight Eisenhower. Her photograph appeared in newspapers and on the cover of magazines as America's "Woman of the Year." She even danced on television many times.

President Eisenhower

A young man who became her partner admitted he was afraid of dancing with the great Maria Tallchief. "I don't bite, you know," Maria told him.

"Miss Tallchief," he answered, "I'm not afraid of you biting me. I am afraid I'll knock you off pointe."

Maria laughed. "You're not strong enough to knock me off pointe!"

One man, however, did sweep Maria off her feet. His name was Henry Paschen. Everyone called him Buzz. He was not a dancer. He had never even been to a ballet. Once he saw Maria perform in *Firebird*, however, he could not take his eyes from her. Maria felt the same attraction. "His sky blue eyes made my heart stop whenever I looked into them," she said. They married in June of 1956.

A few years later, another love came into Maria's life . . . her daughter Elise was born.

"I don't think I'll ever forget the feeling of seeing that beautiful child when they brought her to me for the first time," Maria wrote in her autobiography. "She had black hair, long and silky, and I thought 'She's truly an American-Indian baby.' When I held her in my arms and her eyes looked into mine, I thought 'This is heaven.' "

Days later at home with her new baby, Maria slipped into her toe shoes and laced them. Her father was visiting. He said, "You have a husband and a baby now. You ought to be content."

"I am content, Daddy," she answered.

"Then it's time to put those shoes away for good."

Stop dancing? "Never!" she told her father. "I have to dance."

Joseph Tall Chief knew his daughter was every bit as stubborn as he was. He said nothing more about it.

Maria had everything she had wanted: an exciting career and a beautiful family. Her sister, Marjorie's life seemed enchanted, too. She and her husband had joined the Paris Opera Ballet, and they had twin children. And yet, sadness and loss comes into every life. A few months after Elise was born, Maria's father became dangerously ill. The doctors in Fairfax did not know how to make him well again. Maria turned to the one person who had always been there to help her and who was still a

very dear friend, George Balanchine. "I'm so afraid," she told him.

George was always the calm spot in the center of a storm. He told Maria to bring her father to Chicago and let the doctors there examine him. Maria made all the arrangements. Within days, her father and mother had arrived.

Maria tried to mask her shock at seeing him. Her father had always seemed a giant to her. Now, his body sagged from sickness. His eyes were cloudy. His skin was yellowish. The doctors in Chicago offered little hope. Joseph Tall Chief died in October 1959. As he had wished, his family

buried him in the cemetery in Fairfax among the other Tall Chief graves. Maria's grief ran very deep. Had it only been ten months ago that she had argued with her father about putting away her toe shoes forever? He had been healthy and happy then. Now he was gone.

The death of her father was not Maria's only loss. When Grandma Tall Chief also died, Maria returned again to the small graveyard in Fairfax. An old Osage woman standing near Grandma's grave was chanting. The sound was haunting, familiar and yet mysterious, too. It was the voice of Maria's people from long, long ago. Perhaps as

Maria walked away from the cemetery, she took some comfort in knowing that her father and her Grandma were together again.

For many months, Maria mourned. Even though her grief exhausted her, she still laced up her toe shoes and danced. And in her dancing, she slowly began to heal.

Chapter 11
The Protest

Maria found joy in the music and movement of her body. She wanted to share that joy with others, especially children. When a television star named Dave Garroway invited Maria to perform a dance recital for an audience of American-Indian children, Maria quickly said yes. Here was an opportunity

for Princess Wa-Xthe-Thonba to bring together the two worlds in which she lived—the world of ballet and the world of Native Americans. Because the program would be on TV, many thousands of people across the country would see the performance.

The 1960s was a time of unrest. Across the country, people were joining hands to protest unfair treatment of people of color. African Americans marched side by side with white protesters to demand equal rights for *all* Americans.

Native Americans, too, were protesting. Many believed that images of American Indians on television and in movies were prejudiced. Those images portrayed their people as uncivilized and savage.

On the afternoon of Maria's television show, the school buses that were to bring the children to

the auditorium did not arrive. Maria stood on stage in costume, but the seats were empty.

"Where is everybody?" Dave Garroway asked.

He was angry but also worried. He had a television program to broadcast, and he had no audience.

"Wait a while," someone suggested. "They'll come."

An hour later, the auditorium was still dark and silent. The children never came.

Maria danced that afternoon for the television cameras only. Perhaps for the first time ever, she danced without joy in her heart. "I was disappointed by the experience, and sorry that the children didn't return for the telecast," Maria said.

Later, she learned what had happened. Some Native Americans in the Chicago area refused to

bring the children to the auditorium. They thought the television people were trying to steal away their native culture, trying to make their children more American and less Native American.

Maria was deeply hurt. She believed it was possible to live in two worlds. She had done it. Her sister Marjorie had done it. But most of all, Maria believed this: "The beauty of ballet should not be denied to anyone."

Chapter 12
The Swans

When Maria was forty-one years old, she realized her time in the spotlight was ending. She was watching a young dancer in rehearsal lift her leg higher and higher. The dancer's balance was off, and Maria corrected her. The girl was so eager to please, so hungry to learn. Maria thought with surprise, *Why, that was me a lifetime ago!*

Practically all her life, Maria had been dancing. If she stopped, what would she do? A whole new generation of young girls were just now tying on their toe shoes for the first time. Perhaps she could teach them what Madame Nijinska and George Balanchine had taught her—passion and discipline.

Still, the thought of being "retired" frightened her. Backstage, whenever she had felt nervous, Maria had lifted her chin and stepped forward to show the world what she could do. Was it time now to show the world again what she could do as a teacher?

The decision tormented Maria. "Should I . . . or shouldn't I?" she asked herself over and over again. When Elise was younger, Maria took her on tour with her. In the hotel rooms late at night, Elise set out plates of food for her mother. Sometimes, if she wasn't too tired after a performance, Maria draped a silk scarf over the lamp to create a soft glow, and she read to Elise. Once, Elise had written a poem that began:

Because she is my mother,
every night she turns into Cinderella.

After the final performance of a tour in Venezuela in 1966, Maria returned to her hotel room alone. Buzz and Elise were not waiting in the wings. They were home in Chicago. Maria longed to be with them. That night, she made up her mind. It was time she stopped turning into Cinderella.

A few days later, Maria returned to her family in Chicago and left the stage for good. She began to build a new life for herself. She made a studio on the top floor of her house and gave herself lessons each day. She began to work with performers at the Chicago Lyric Opera and later, helped to begin the Chicago City Ballet. All

along, she never lost touch with her closest friend, George Balanchine.

In 1983, Maria received a frightening telephone call. George was in the hospital. Maria flew to New York City. As she hurried down the hall toward George's hospital room, Maria felt as if her life was about to change again. George had created a golden age of ballet in America, and she had been part of it. "I couldn't imagine the world without him," she confessed.

Maria entered the room and drew a chair close to his bedside. George was too weak to sit up, but he smiled when he saw Maria. A short while later, the nurse asked her to leave. Maria knew she would never see George again.

Soon after George died, Maria wrote, "The ballet world in which I grew up is gone."

In the years that followed, Maria found joy in new experiences: her daughter's success as a writer, walks along Lake Michigan in Chicago or along the beach in Florida. Although she no longer performed publicly after 1966, she never put away her toe shoes. Each day, she gave herself a class at the barre. Sometimes she taught.

When Maria was seventy-one years old, the Kennedy Center in Washington, D.C., named her "one of the outstanding artists of the twentieth century." Many in the world of ballet believed Maria Tallchief had achieved her goal of becoming a perfect prima ballerina. Maria knew she had not. But this no longer troubled her. Perfection, she now believed, was impossible except in nature.

Her father's horses running through a meadow of goldenrod on the reservation—that was perfection.

A grove of blackjack trees looking ghostly in the Oklahoma sunset—that was perfection, too.

Once . . . long, long ago, the voices of trumpeter swans echoed *co-ho, co-ho* across the prairie skies. The ancient Osage admired the trumpeter's graceful beauty and endurance. Migrating south, the huge birds were a spectacular display. They slept with their long, curved necks tucked under

their feathers. Then suddenly, they beat their wings and lifted into the sky again to continue their journey.

Sadly, by the time Maria was a child growing up on the reservation, the trumpeters were all but gone. Maria had never seen one. The swans Maria knew were from the fairy tales she danced. In the world of ballet, swans were part-bird, part-woman. They lived in two worlds.

So had Maria.

TIMELINE OF MARIA'S LIFE

1925 —— Maria is born, January 24, in Fairfax, Oklahoma

1926 —— Maria's sister Marjorie is born

1933 —— The Tall Chief family moves to Los Angeles

1937 —— Maria begins dance lessons with Madame Nijinska

1940 —— Madame Nijinska stages *Chopin Concerto*
Maria is cast as one of the *corps*

1942 —— Maria goes to New York City and joins the Ballet Russe

1943 —— Maria performs as soloist in *Chopin Concerto* with the
Ballet Russe; George Balanchine joins the Ballet Russe
as the new choreographer

1946 —— Maria marries George Balanchine in New York City

1949 —— Maria thrills audiences with her performance in *Firebird*

1951 —— Maria and George's marriage ends

1956 —— Maria marries Henry Paschen

1959 —— Maria's daughter Elise is born; Maria's father dies

1966 —— Maria retires from performing

1983 —— George Balanchine dies

1996 —— Maria receives the Kennedy Center Honors

1997 —— Maria publishes her autobiography

1999 —— Maria receives a National Medal of the Arts &
Humanities from president Bill Clinton

Timeline of The World

John Baird transmits recognizable faces in an early form of television	1925
Martha Graham, the American pioneer of the modern-dance revolt, gives her first New York performance	1926
First Mickey Mouse talking film, *Steamboat Willie*, releases	1928
Amelia Earhart makes history as the first woman to fly solo across the Atlantic Ocean	1932
Outbreak of World War II	1939
Attack on Pearl Harbor	1941
World War II ends	1945
Jackie Robinson becomes the first African-American to play Major League Baseball	1947
Segregation by race in schools is unanimously declared unconstitutional by the Supreme Court	1954
Albert Einstein dies	1955
Alaska and Hawaii become the 49th and 50th states	1959
Martin Luther King, Jr. is assassinated	1968
The compact disc or "CD" is launched	1982
Madeleine Albright becomes the first female US Secretary of State	1996
Hong Kong returns to Chinese rule	1997
John F. Kennedy, Jr. dies	1999